Gayatri

Mantram

Coloring Book

--

Vikrmn:

ISBN: 9798863319704
Publisher: MetaVedam
First Edition: 2023

DEDICATED TO...

My son
Viyaan

INTRODUCTION:

The **Gayatri Mantram**, considered as one of the most profound and spiritually significant chants in Sanatan Dharm (also referred to as Hinduism), is a verse from the Rig Veda, an ancient scripture from Bharat (also referred to as India). Comprising 24 syllables it invokes the divine light in the form of a prayer.

Chanted for centuries, its essence transcends religious boundaries, symbolizing the journey from ignorance to knowledge and from darkness to light. Its resonance in the hearts of millions stems from its universal appeal, serving as a timeless reminder of the pursuit of wisdom, truth, and enlightenment.

For over 5,000 years, Sanatan Dharma has cherished the tradition of passing down wisdom through mantras.

However, in today's globalized world, many children and even adults, especially those residing abroad (outside Bharat), lack exposure to these profound teachings. Moreover, technology has seeped into daily life so much that there is hardly any such learning currently being offered.

PURPOSE:

Consider how children are introduced to poetry: through recitation, vibrant images, and colors. Even though they may not fully grasp the meaning, they are captivated. Similarly, this tradition extends to ancient knowledge through Mantras, persisting for millennia.

To ensure this legacy endures, modern approaches are vital. Introducing Mantras to children through activities like coloring, coupled with recitation, provides a contemporary avenue. Just as with poetry, the enchantment lies in the ritual. By blending tradition with creative methods, the profound beauty of Mantras can be embraced by young minds, fostering both understanding and reverence for this timeless spiritual practice.

This initiative seeks to bridge the gap by introducing an innovative approach to learning mantras. By revitalizing this ancient practice in a modern context, it aims to reconnect young minds, even those settled in foreign lands, with the rich heritage of mantra education.

Embracing technology and creative methods, the initiative strives to make these sacred teachings accessible and engaging for the younger generation. Through this endeavor, the age-old wisdom encapsulated in mantras can continue to inspire and guide, ensuring that the spiritual legacy endures in our ever-changing world.

Flip over to explore…

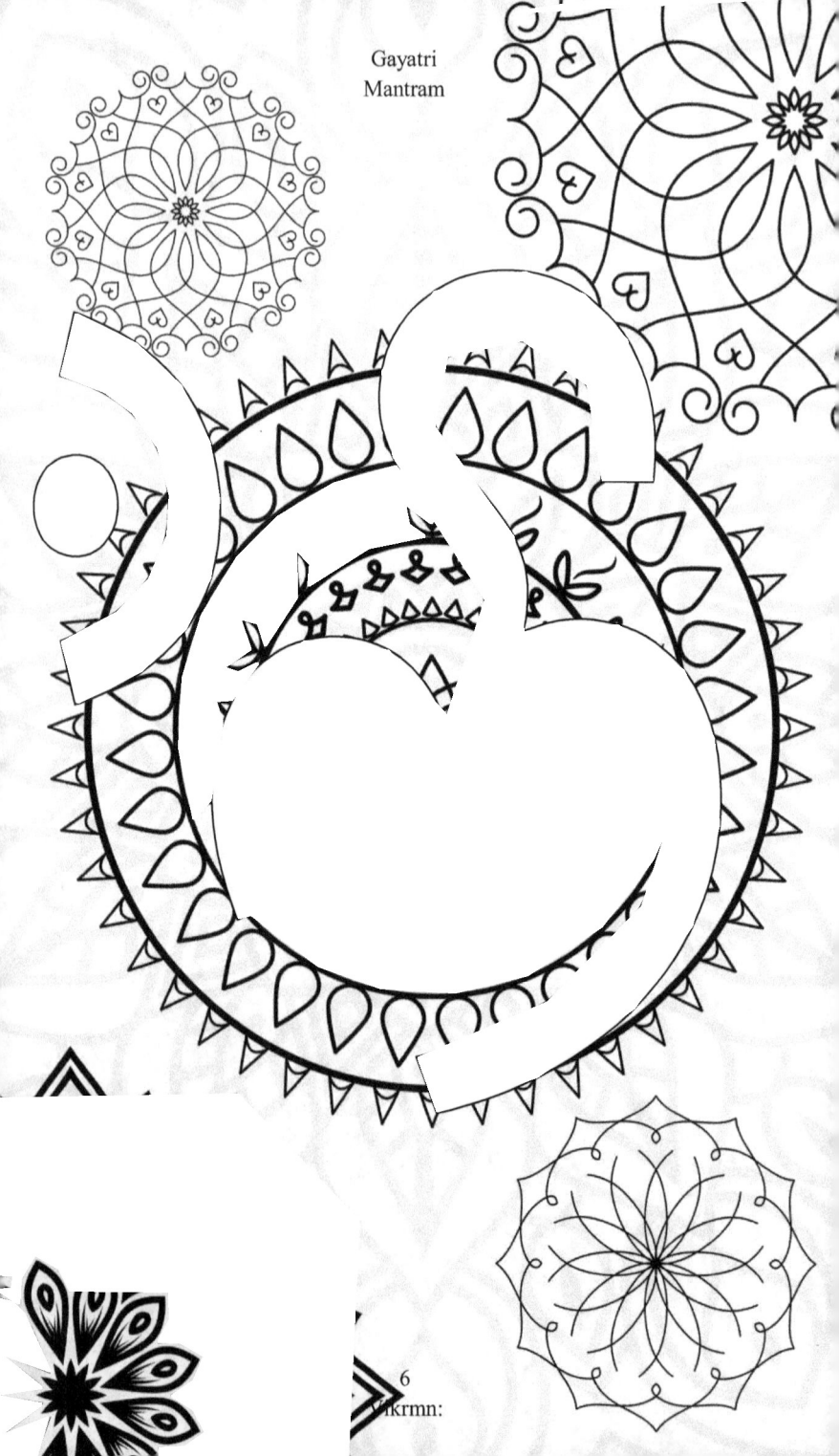

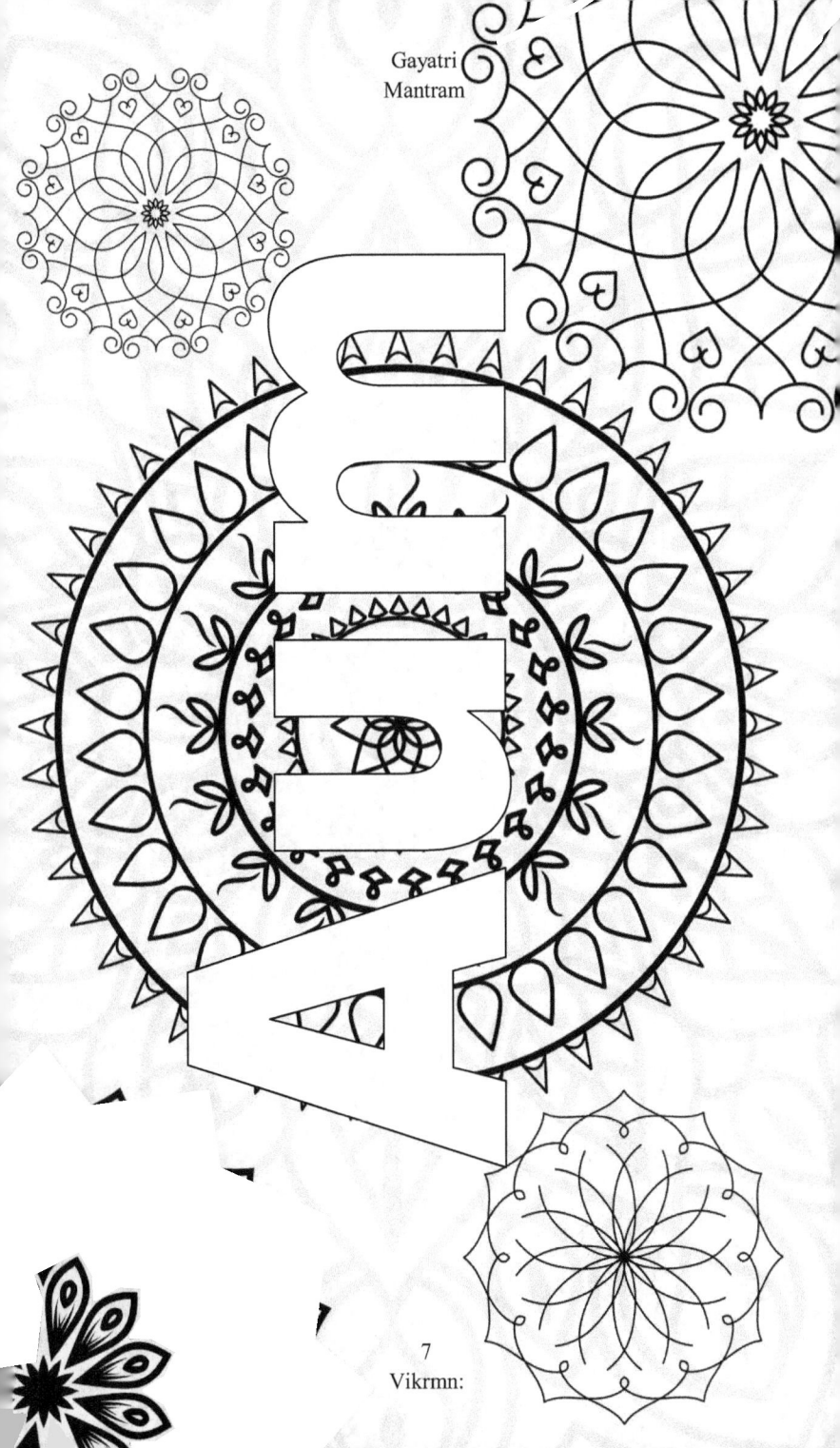

Gayatri
Mantram

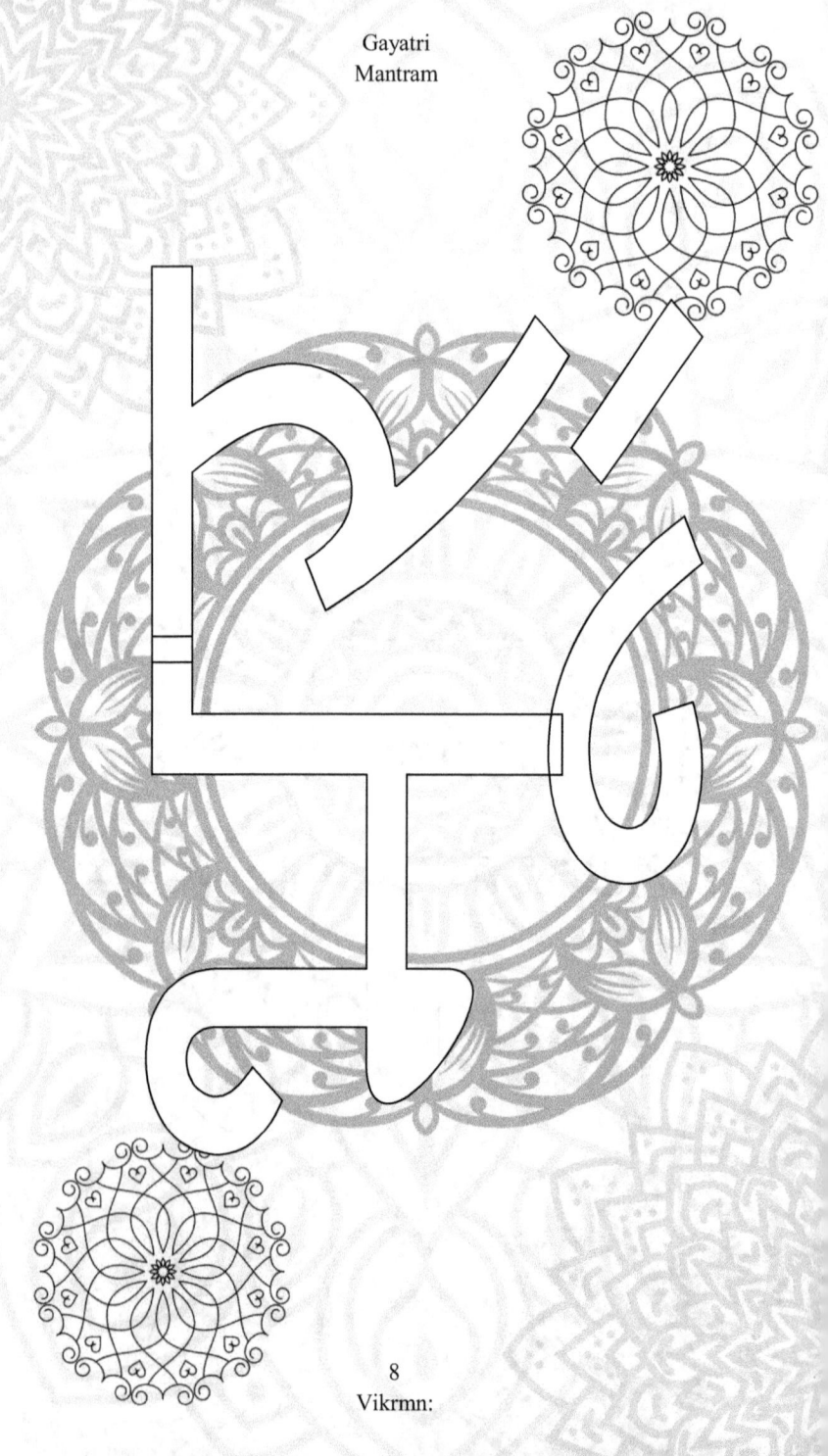

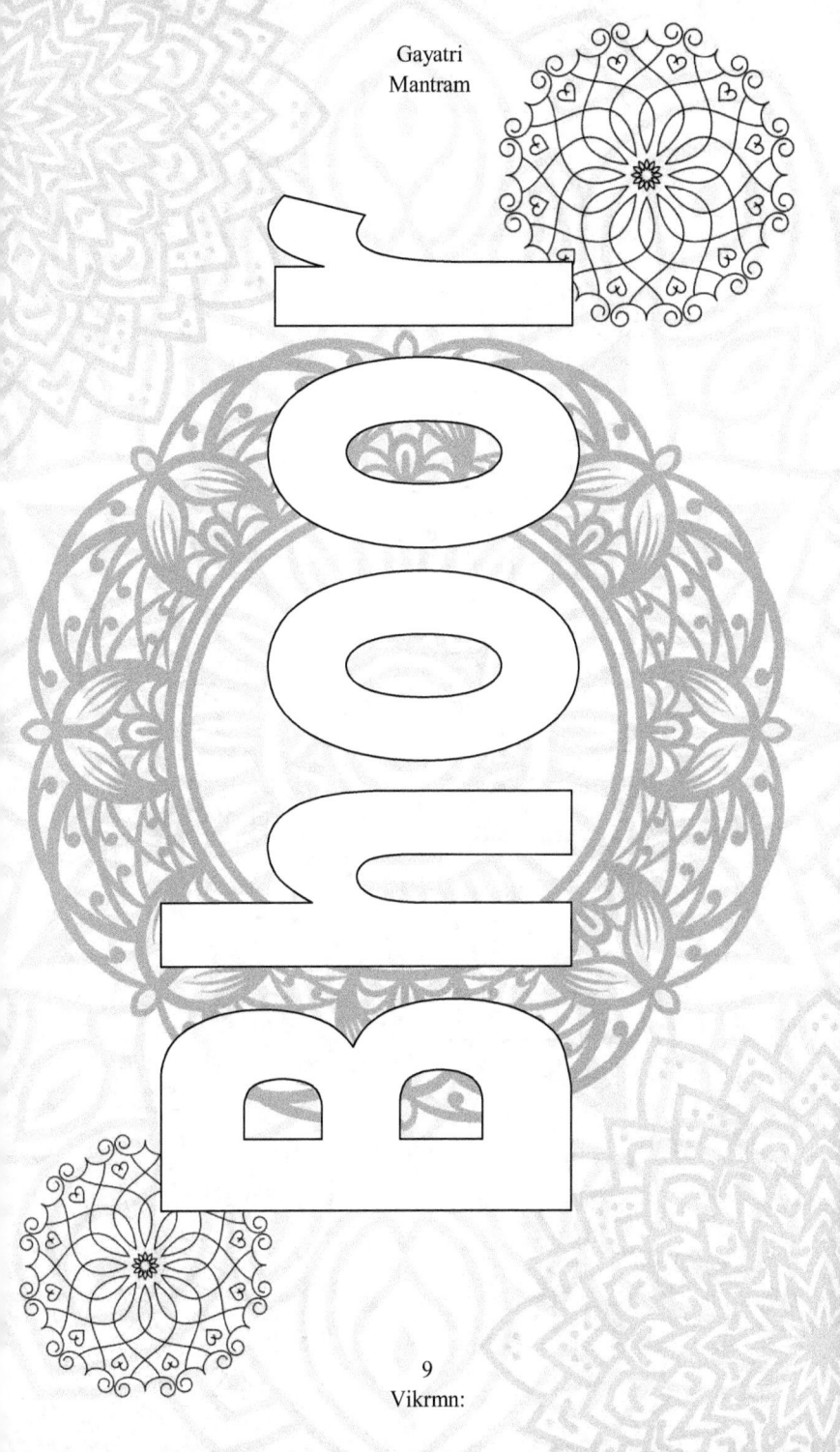

Bhoor

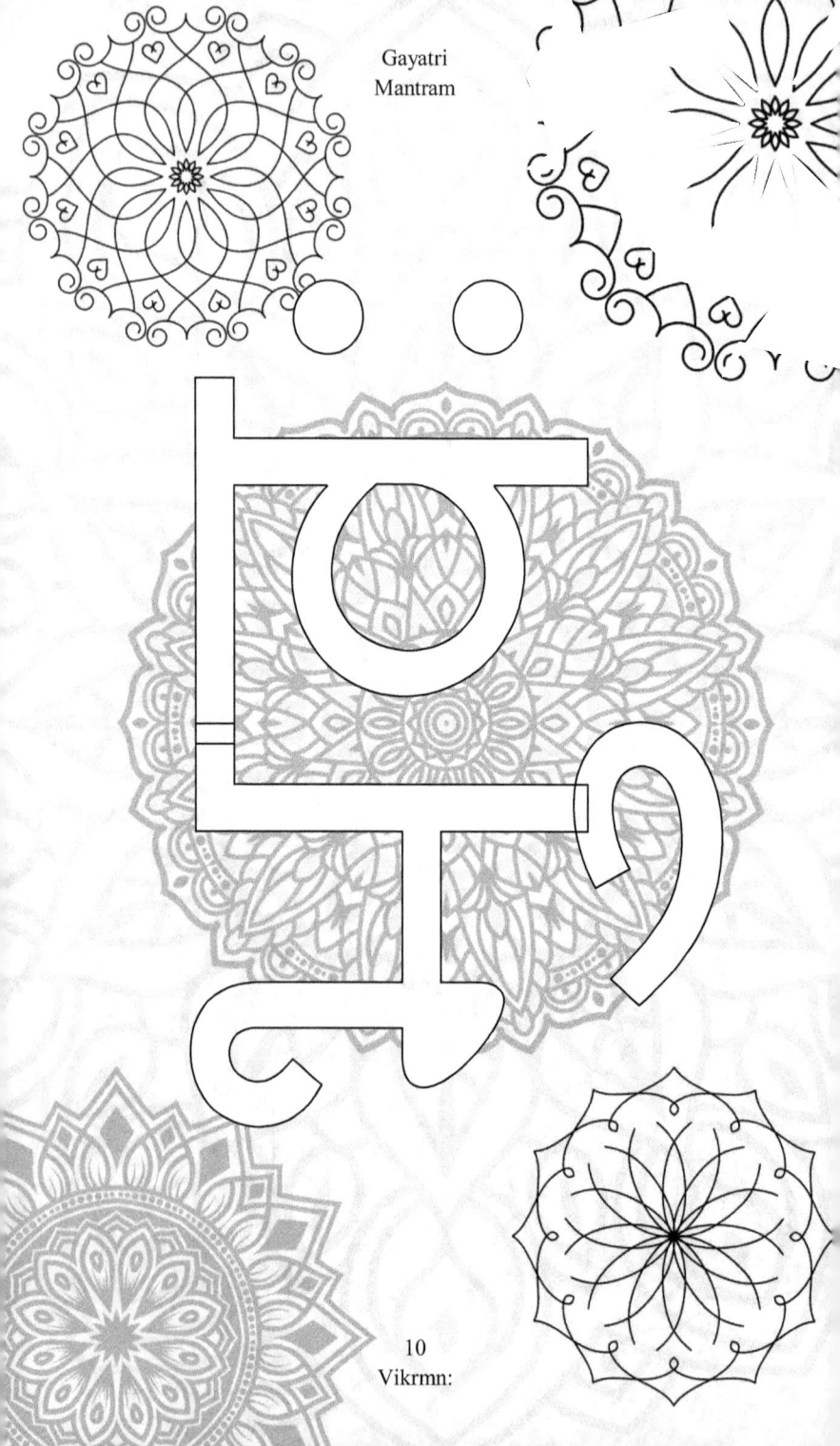

Gayatri
Mantram

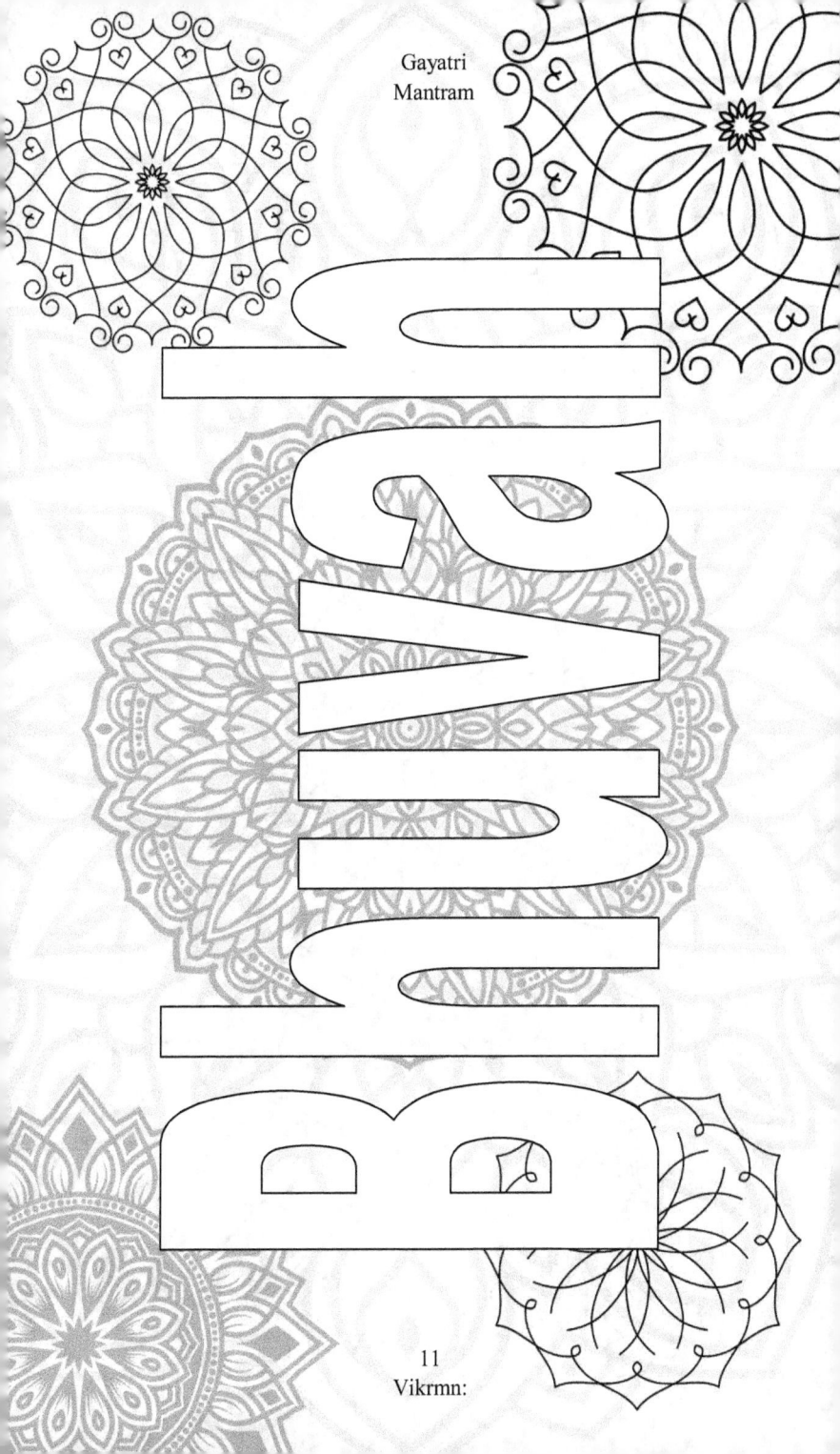

Bhuvah

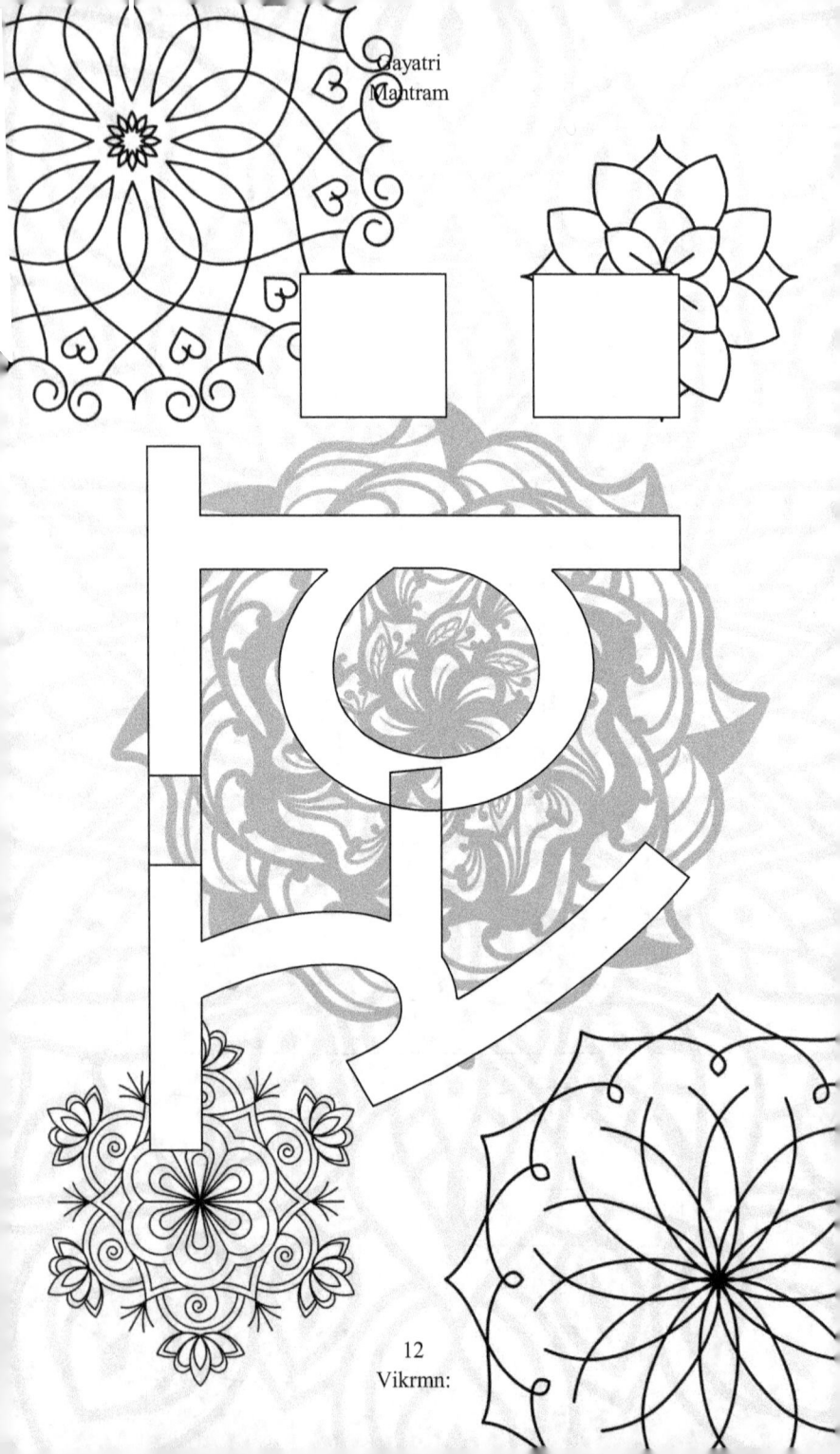

Gayatri
Mantram

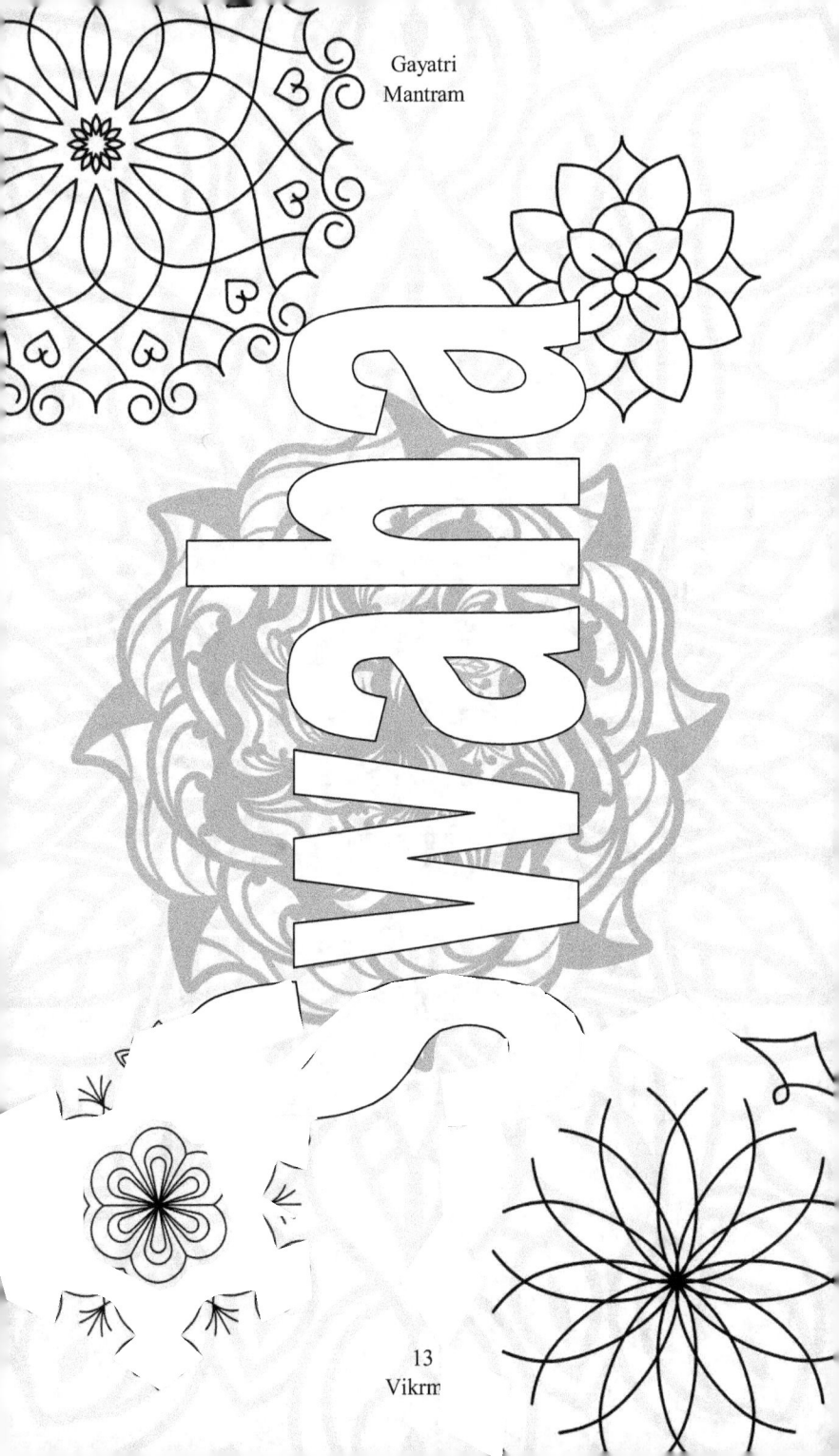

Gayatri
Mantram

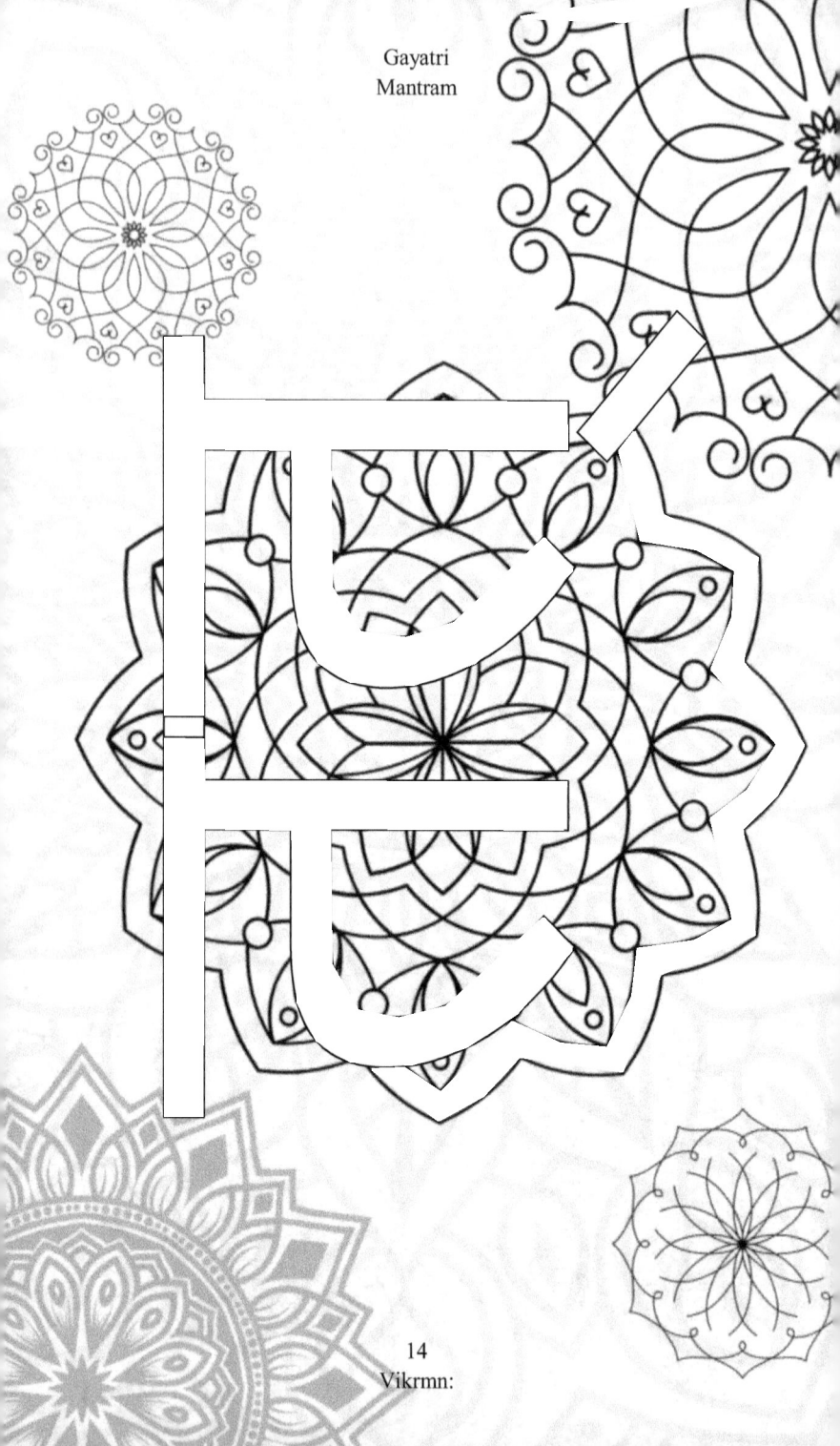

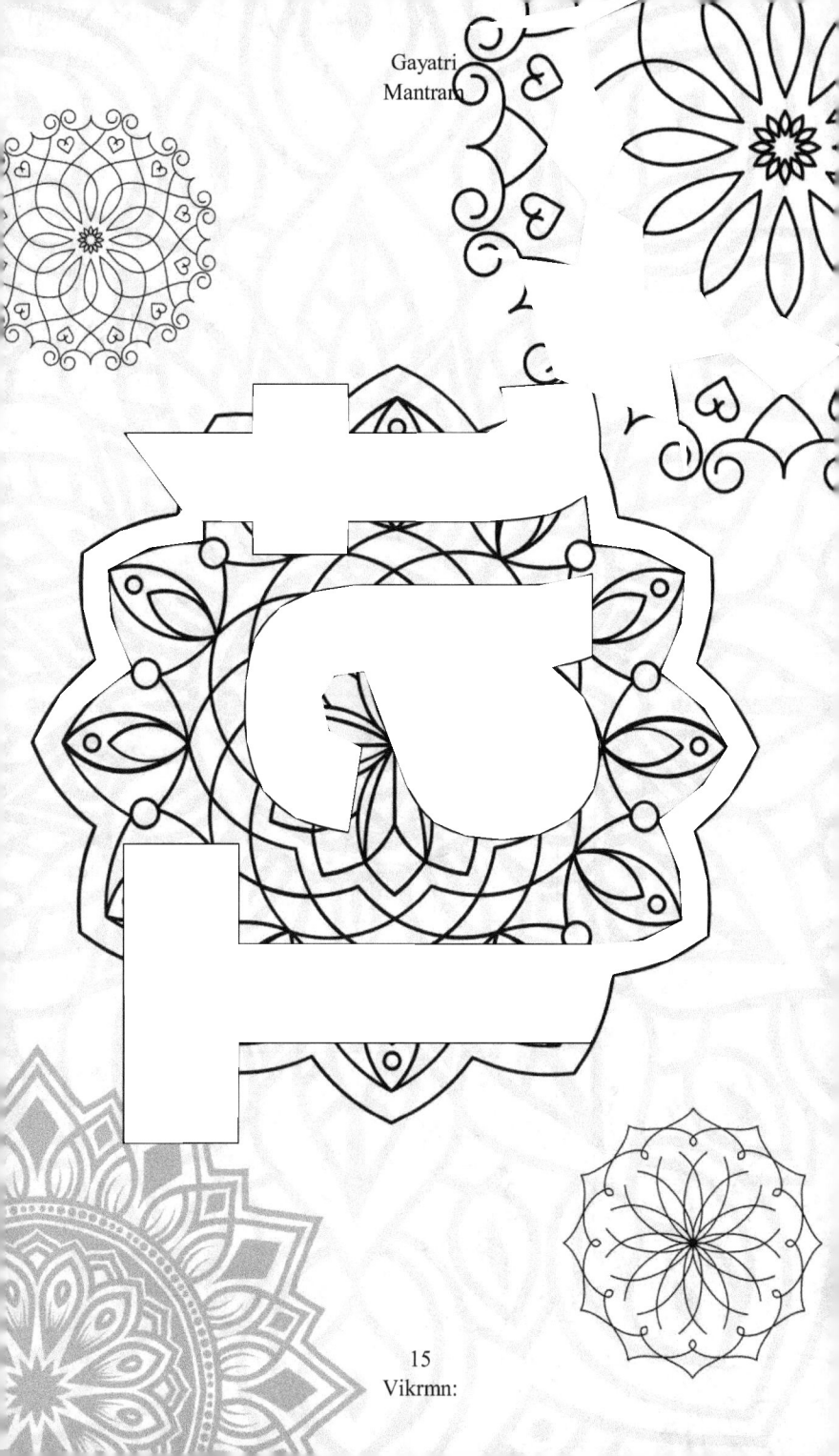

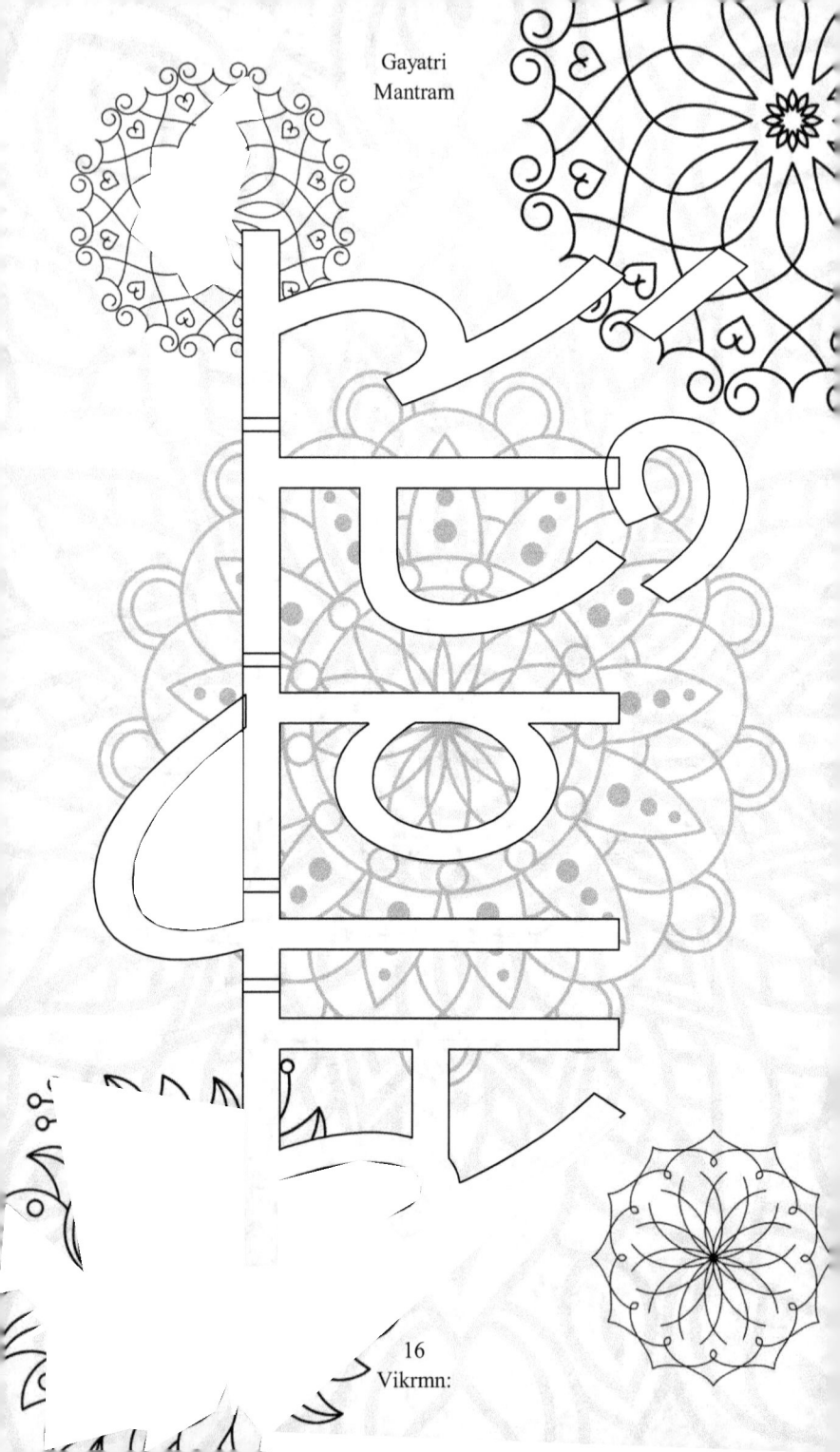

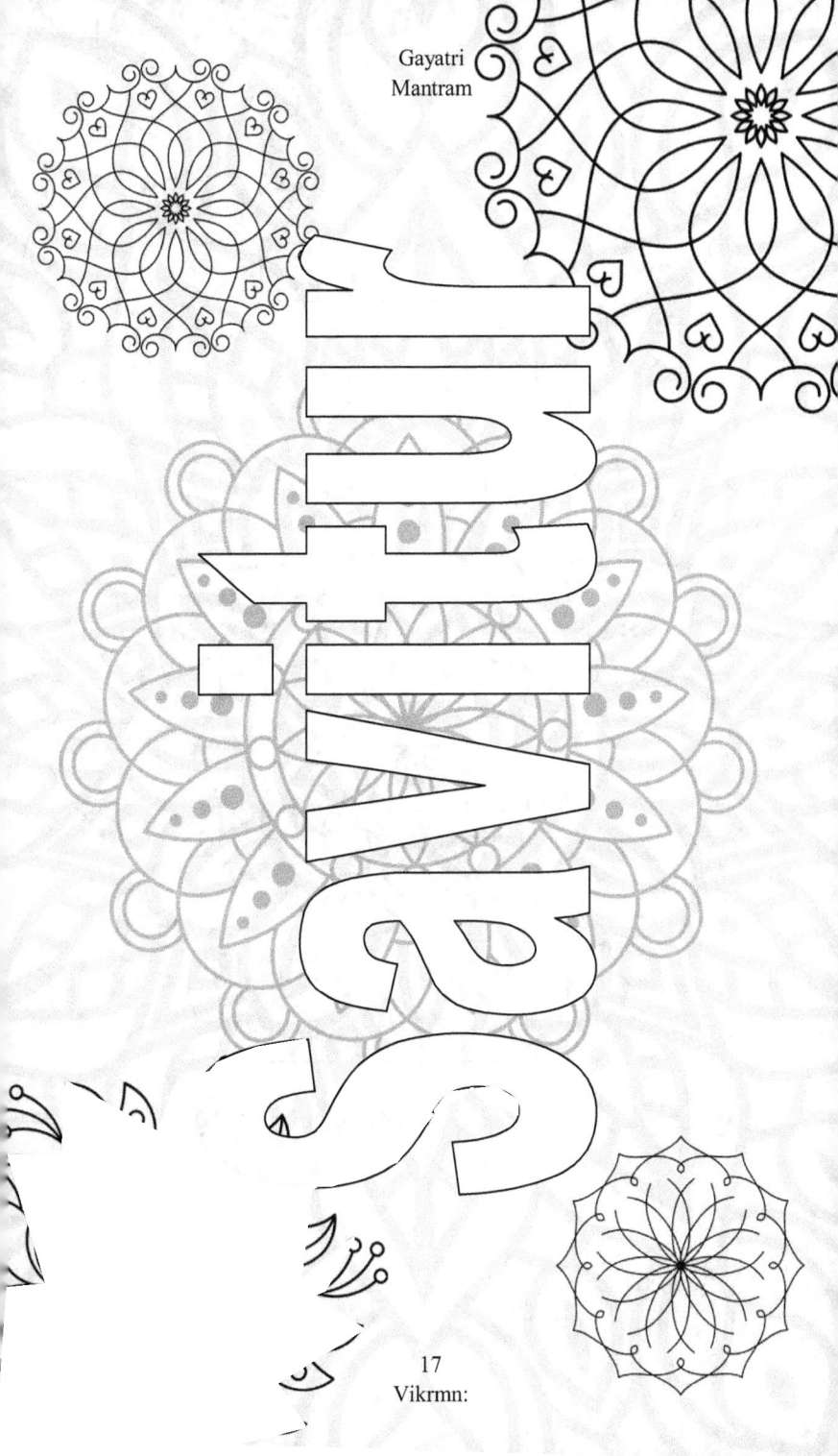

Gayatri
Mantram

Intuitives

17
Vikrmn:

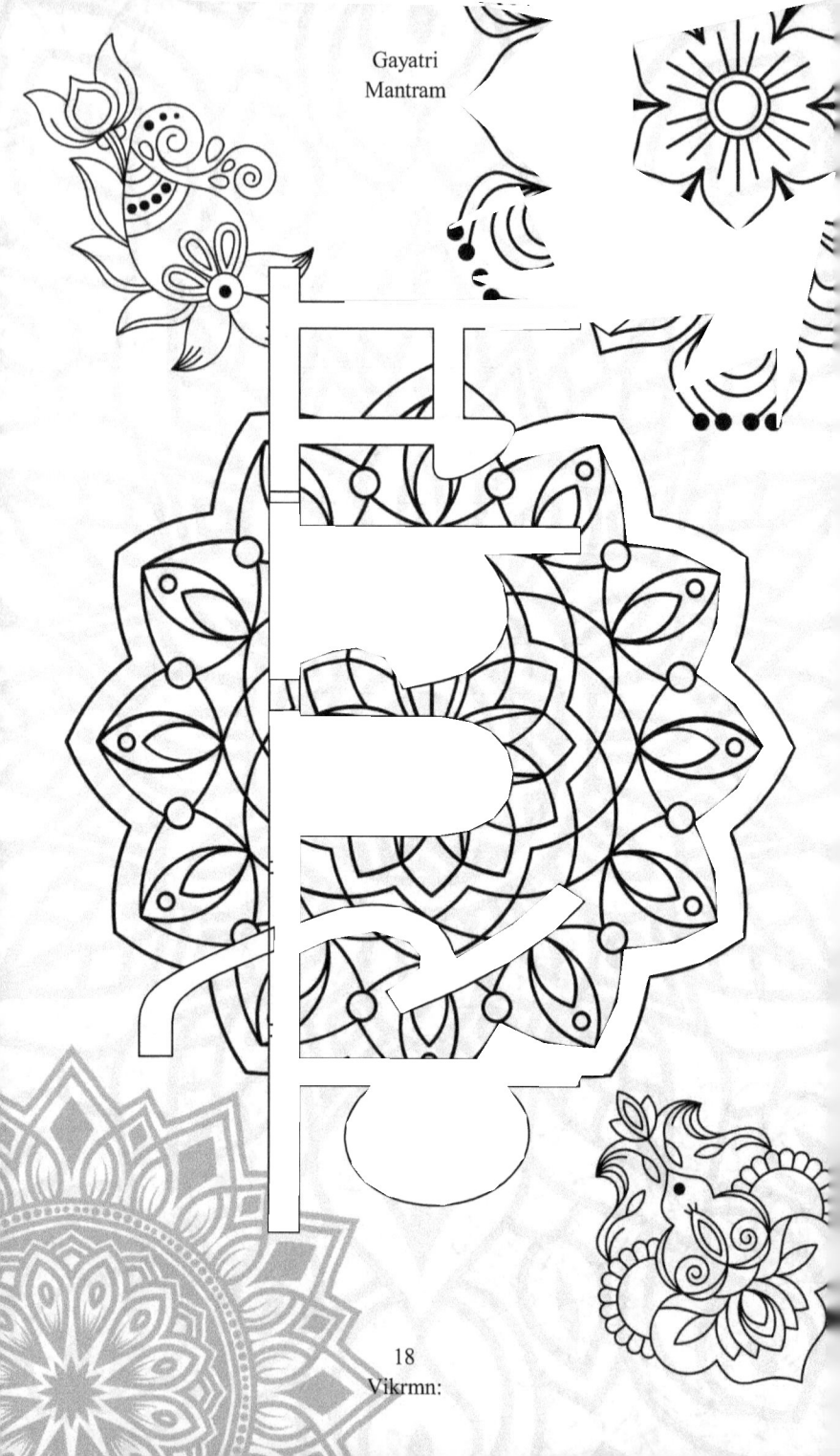

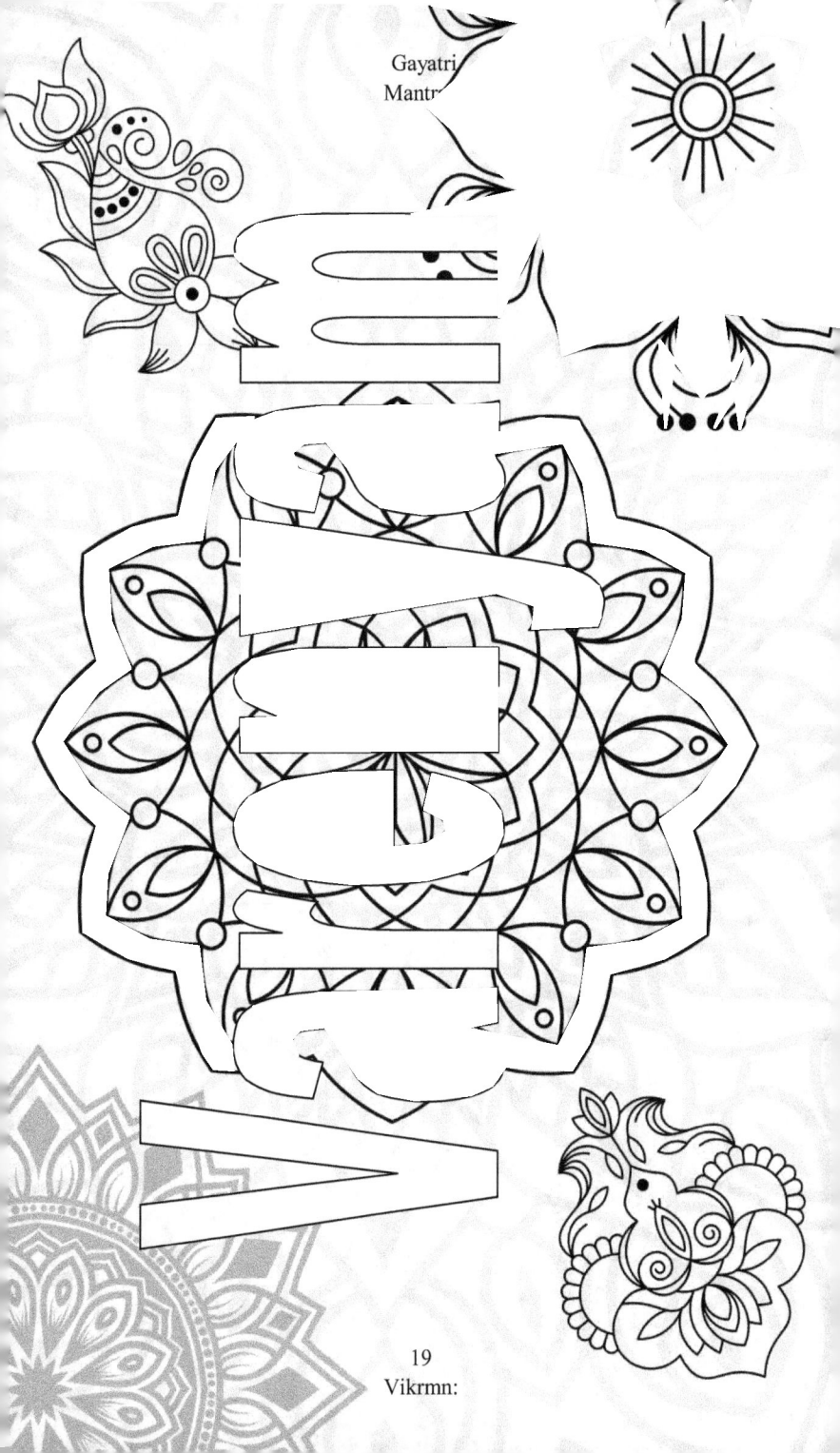

Gayatri
Mantra

Vikrmn:

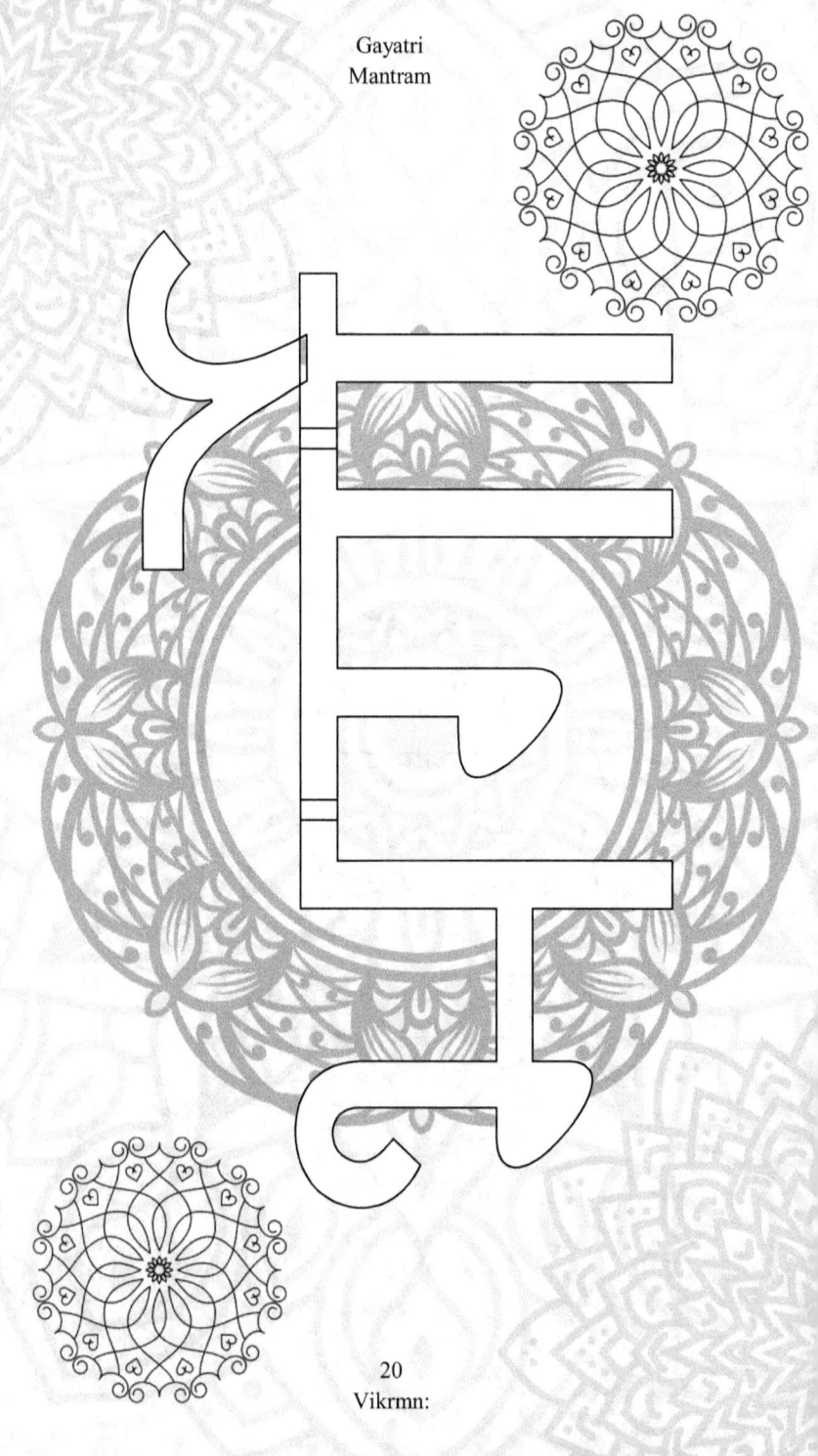

Gayatri
Mantram

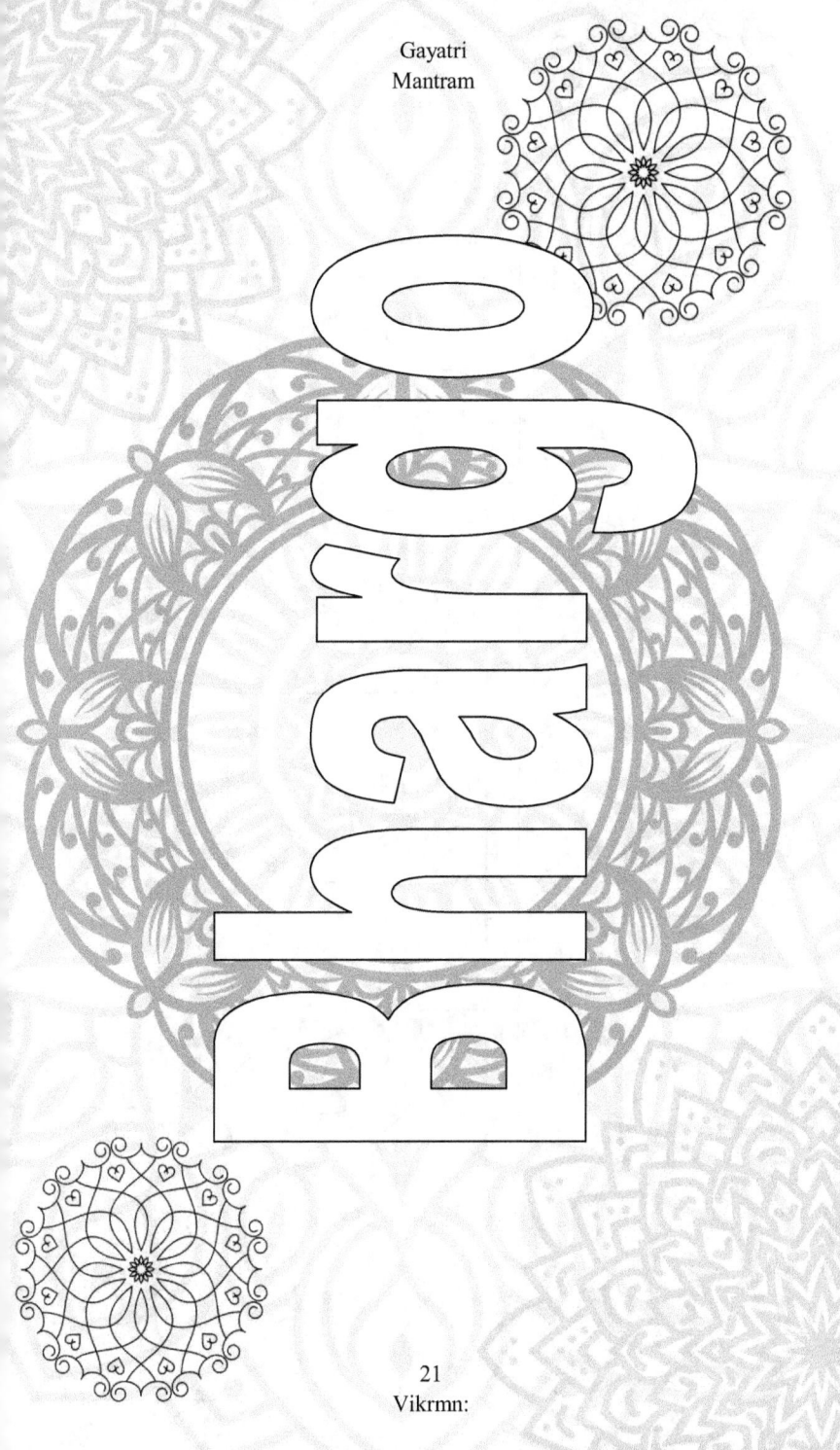

Bhargo

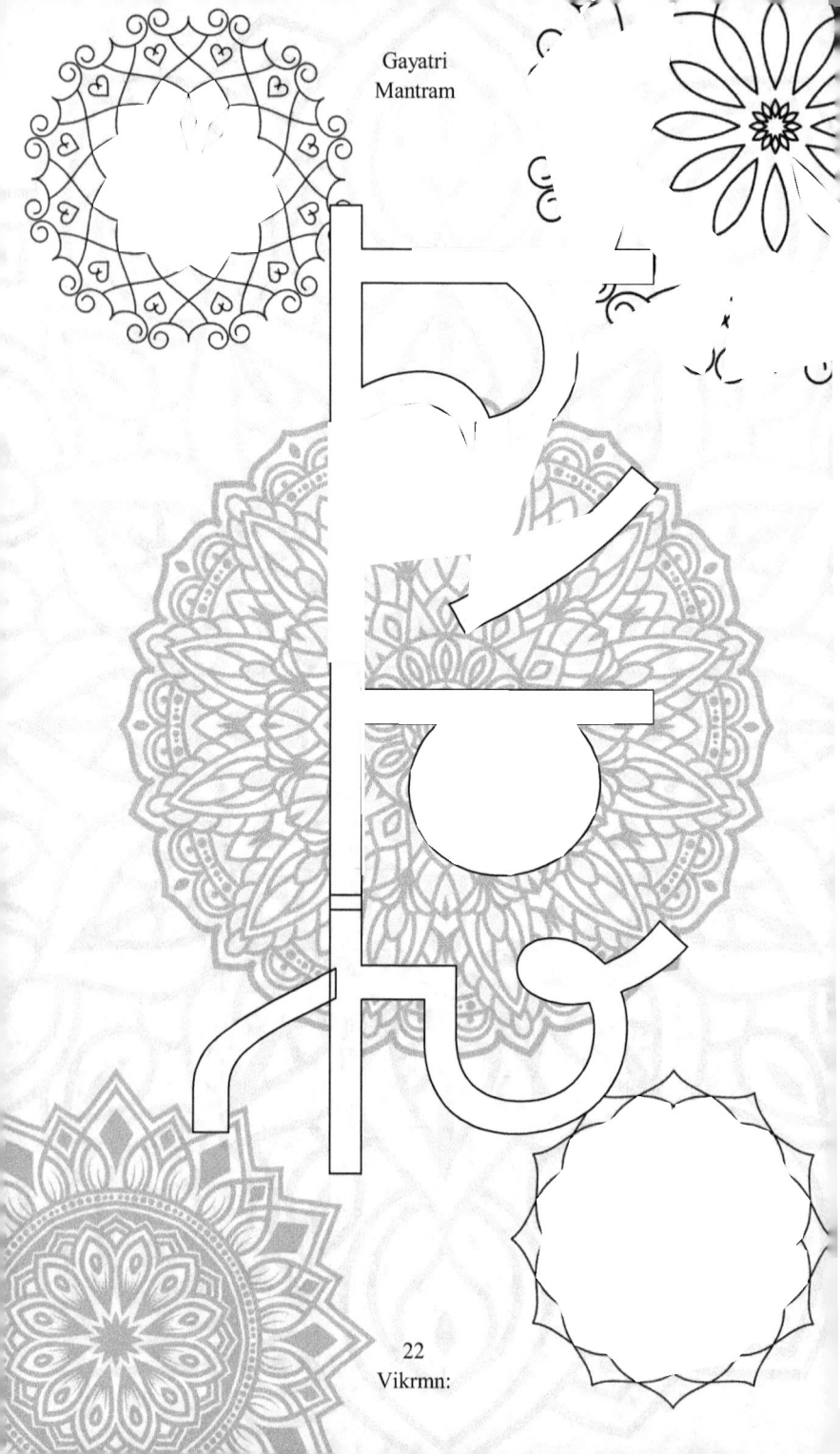

Gayatri
Mantram

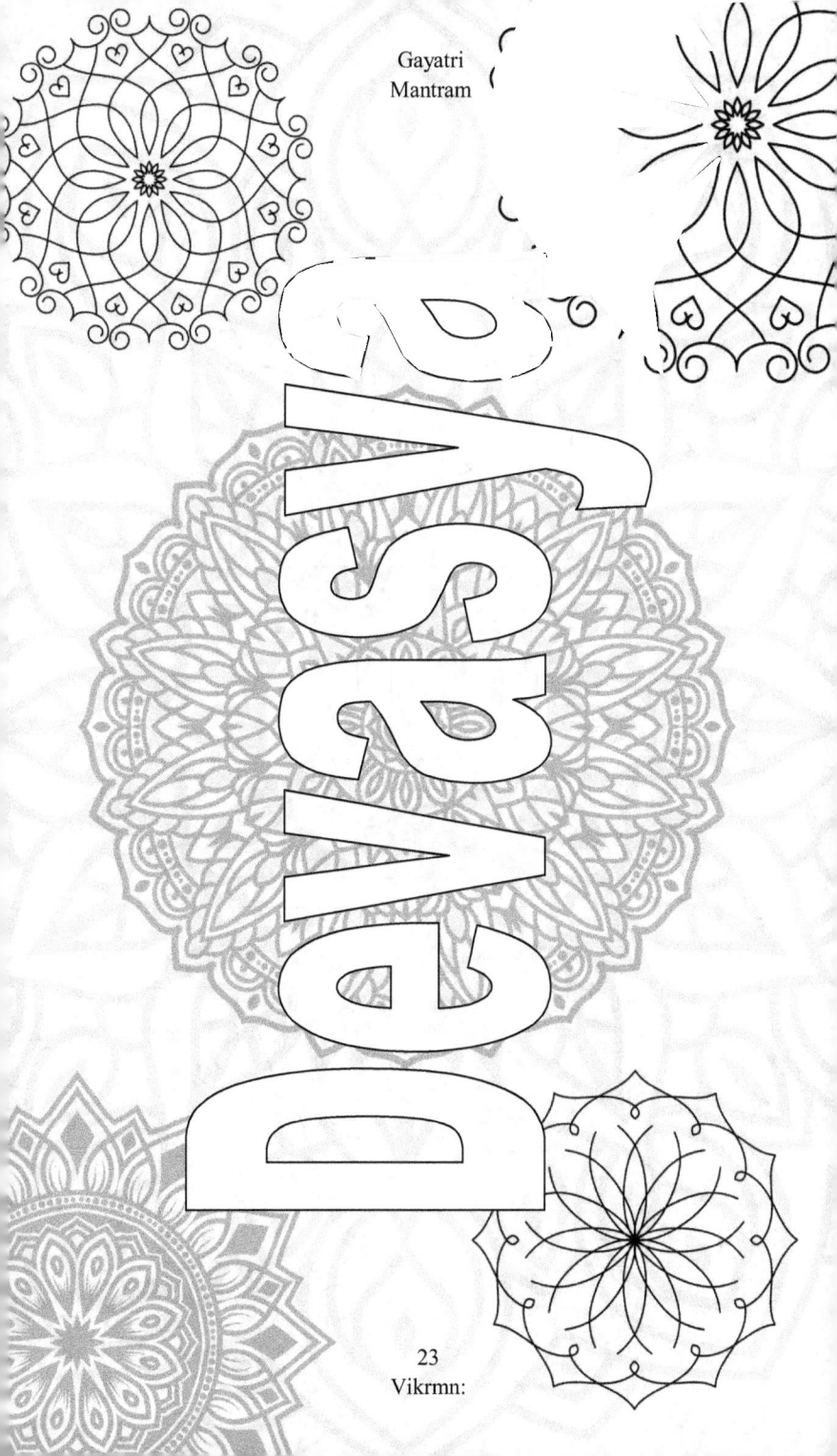

Gayatri
Mantram

Devasy

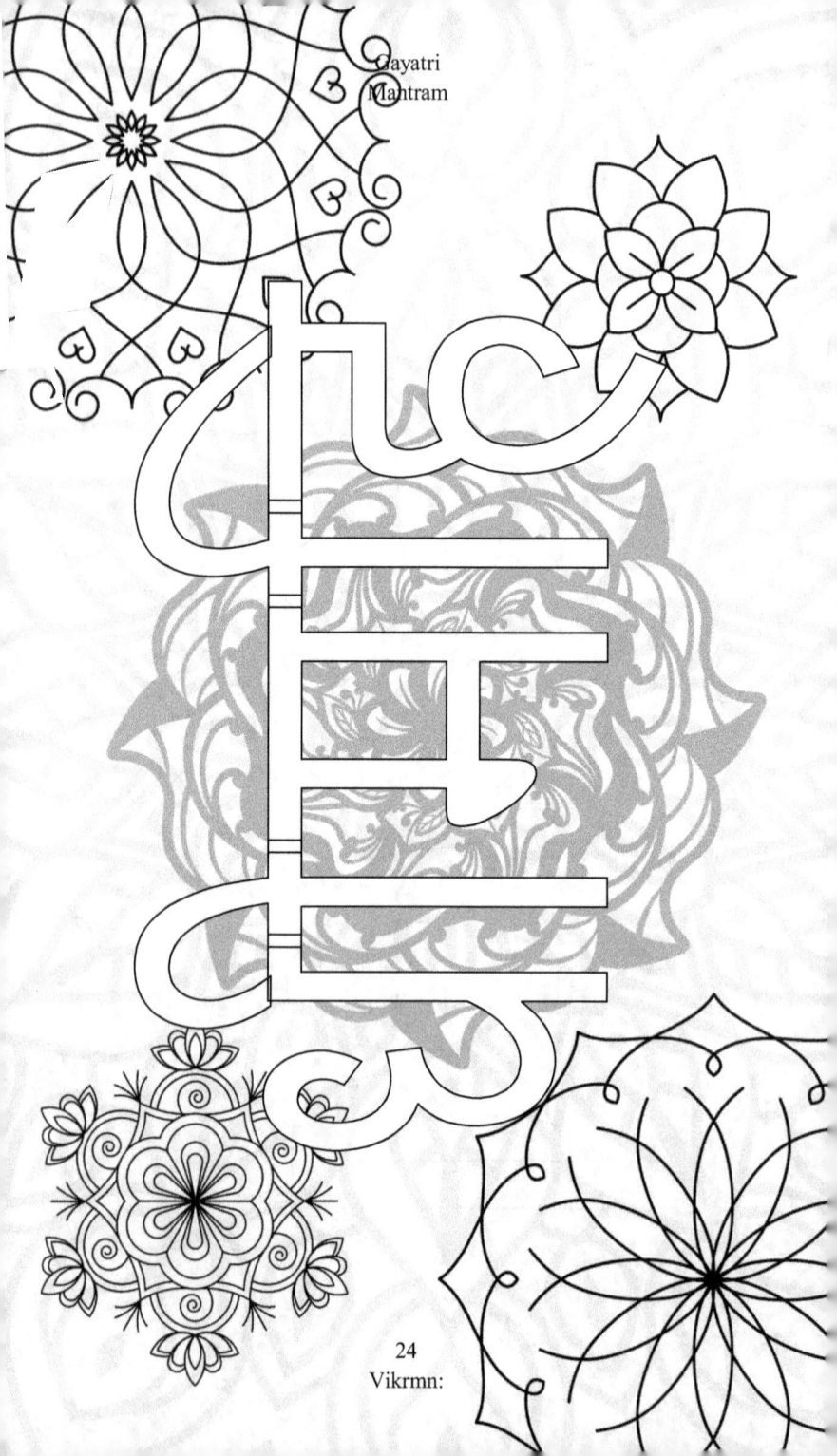

Gayatri
Mahtram

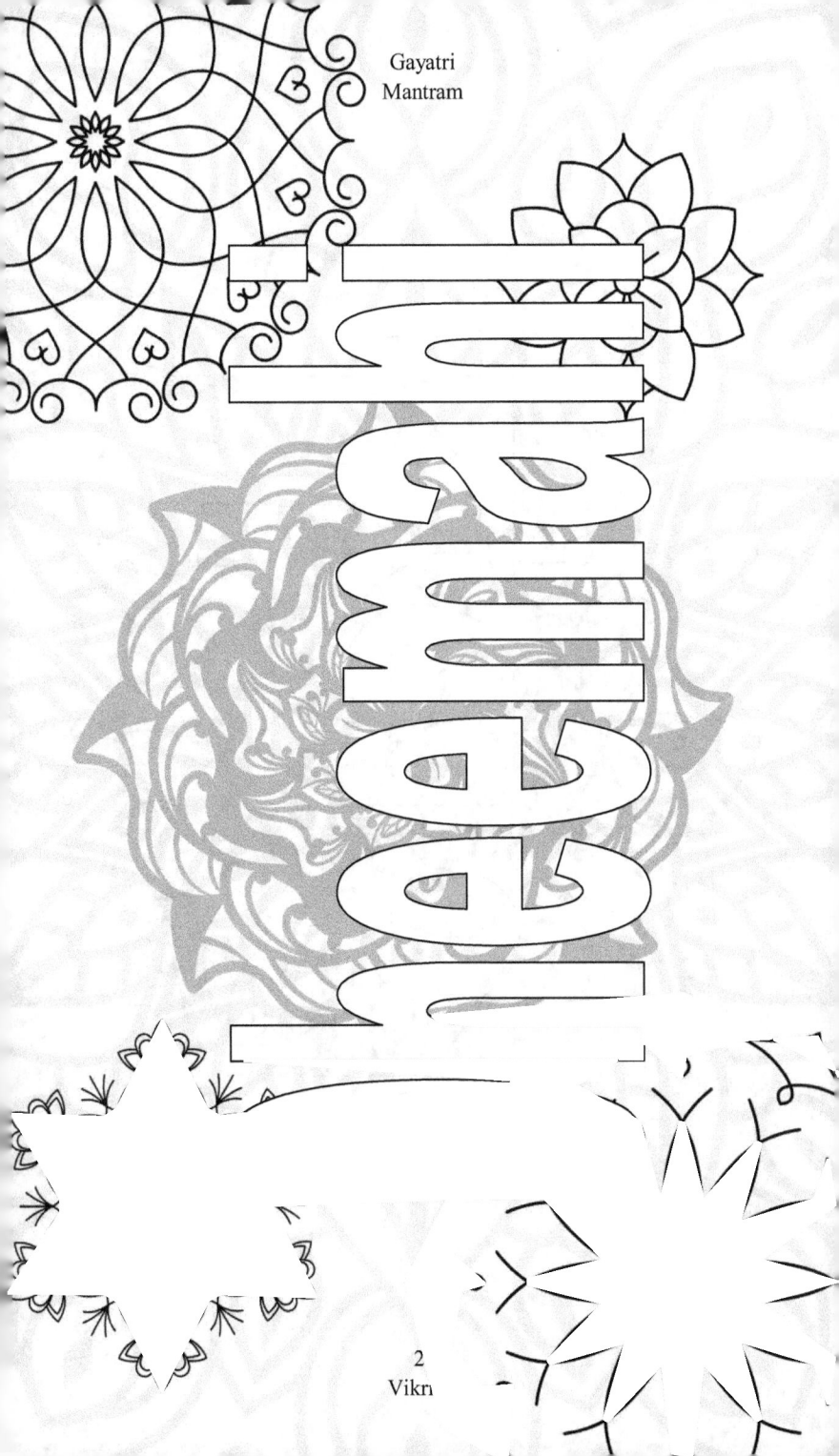

heemahi

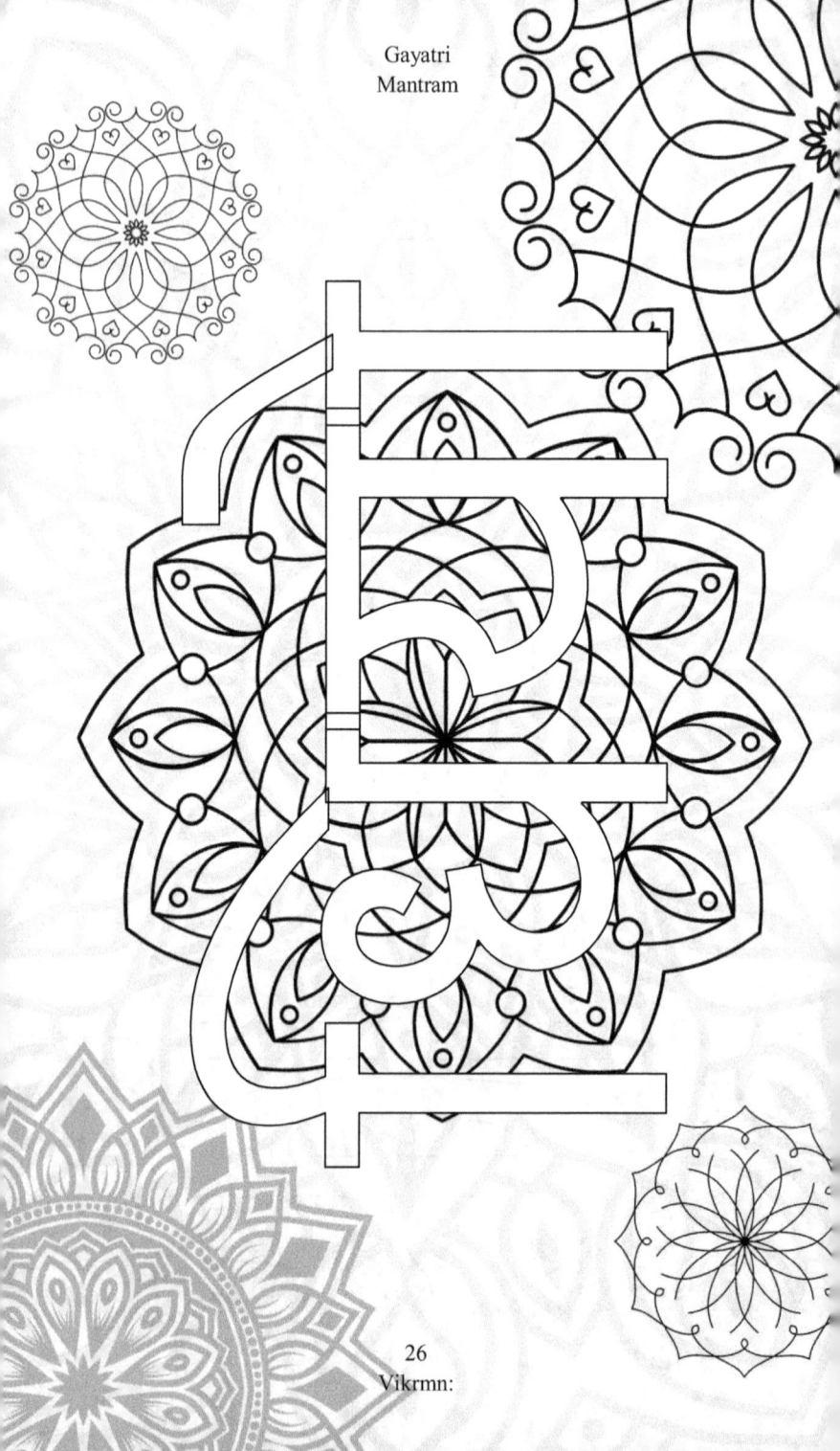

Vikrmn:

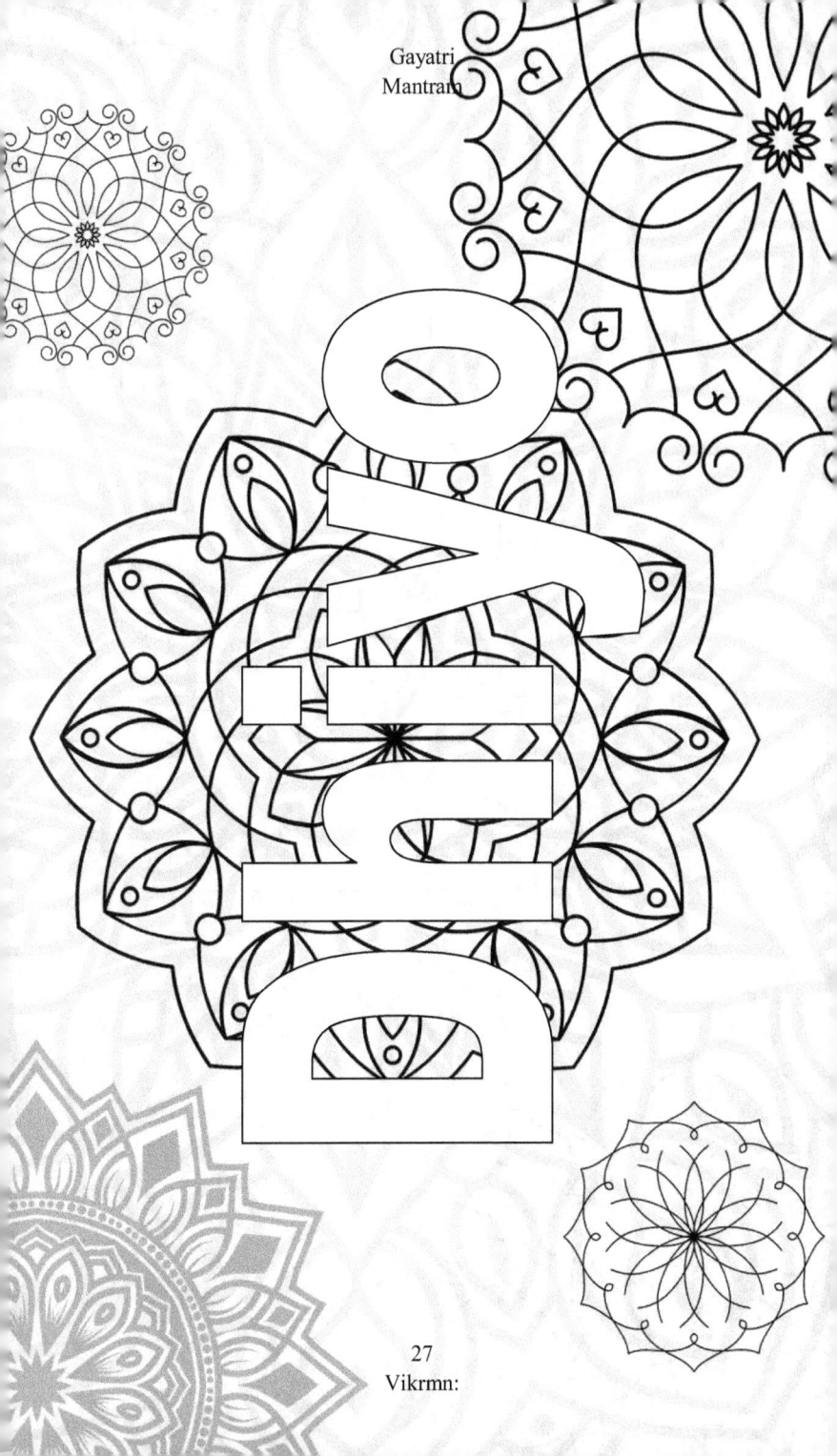

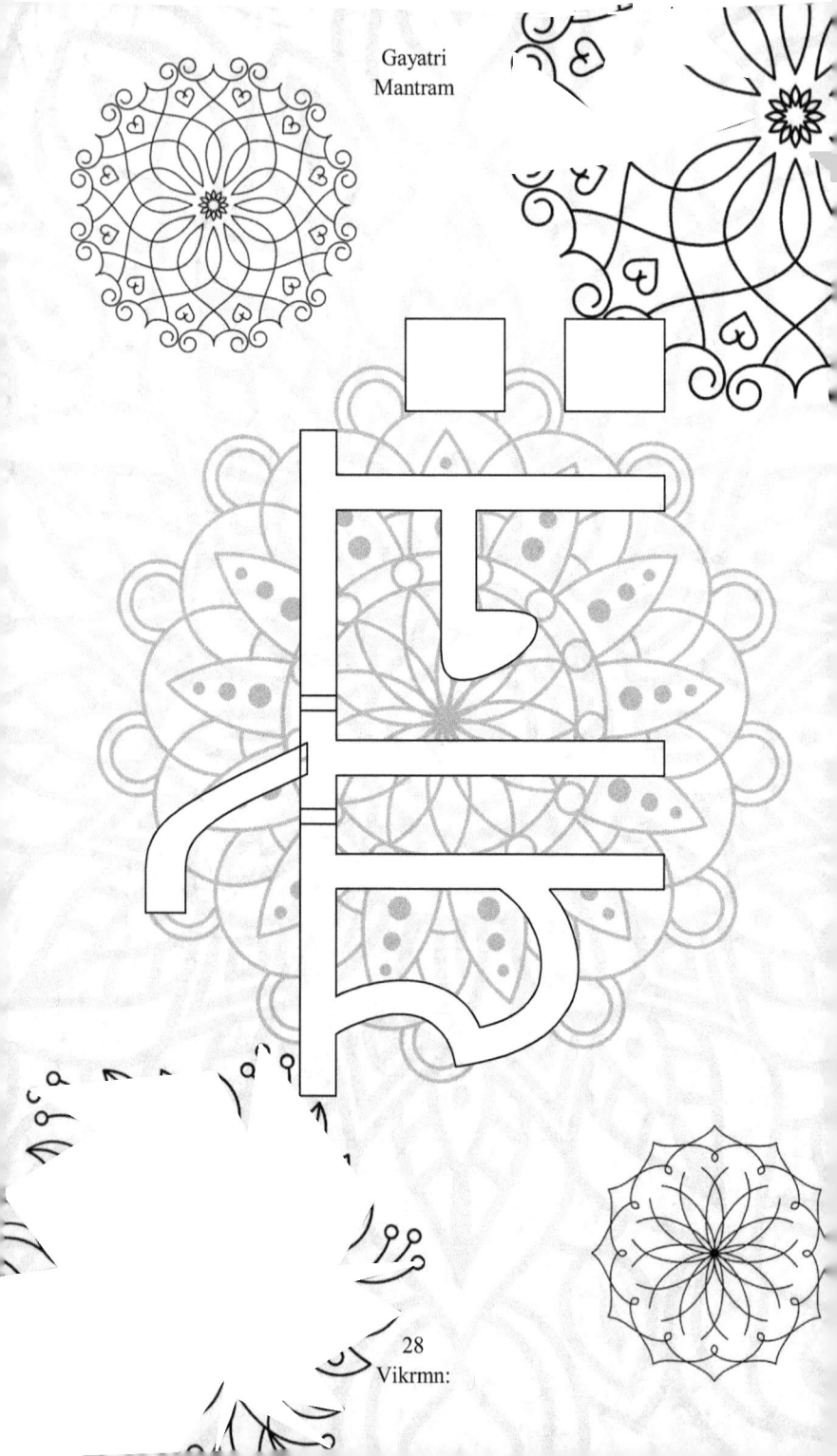

Gayatri
Mantram

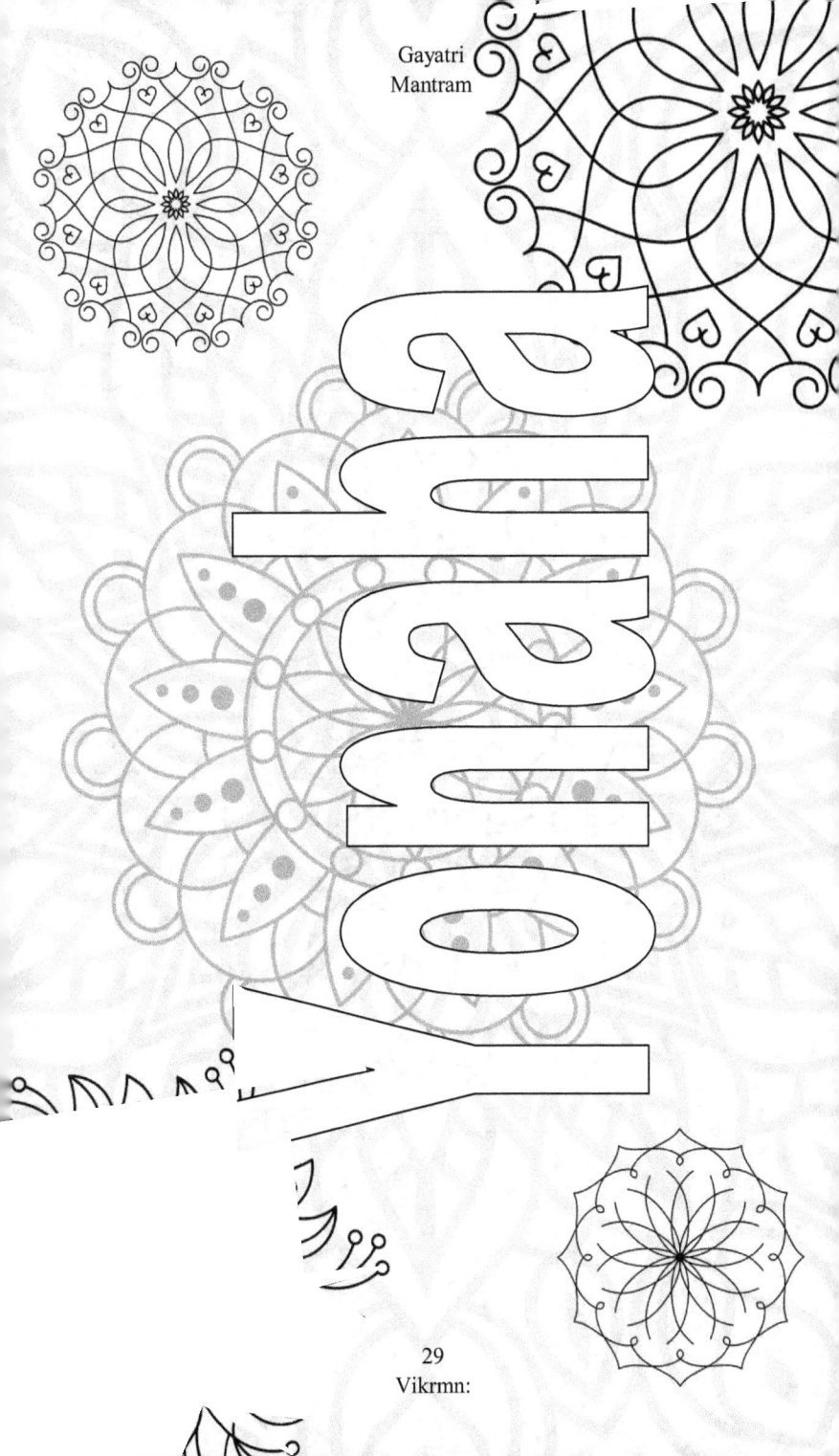

Yohana

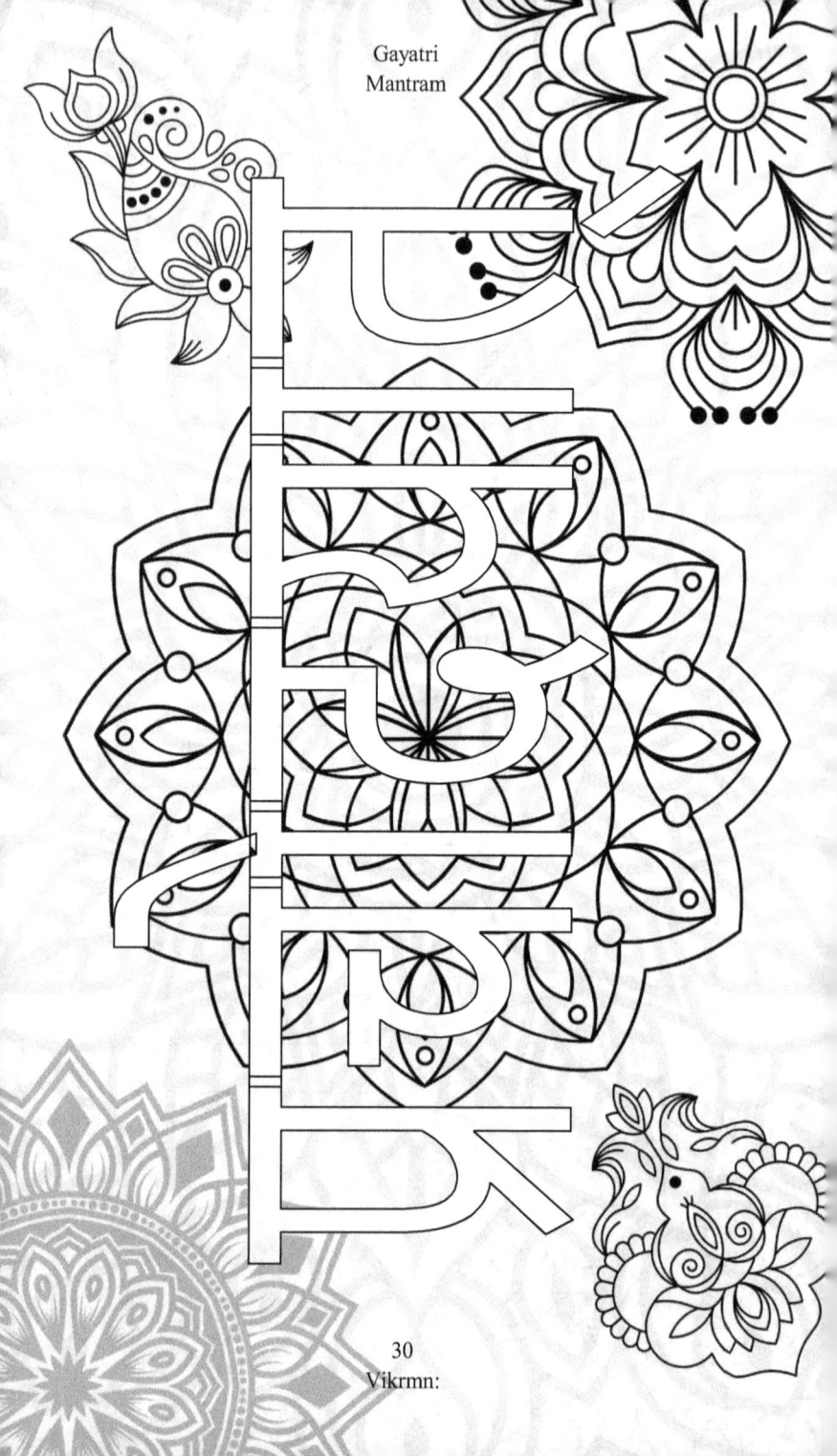

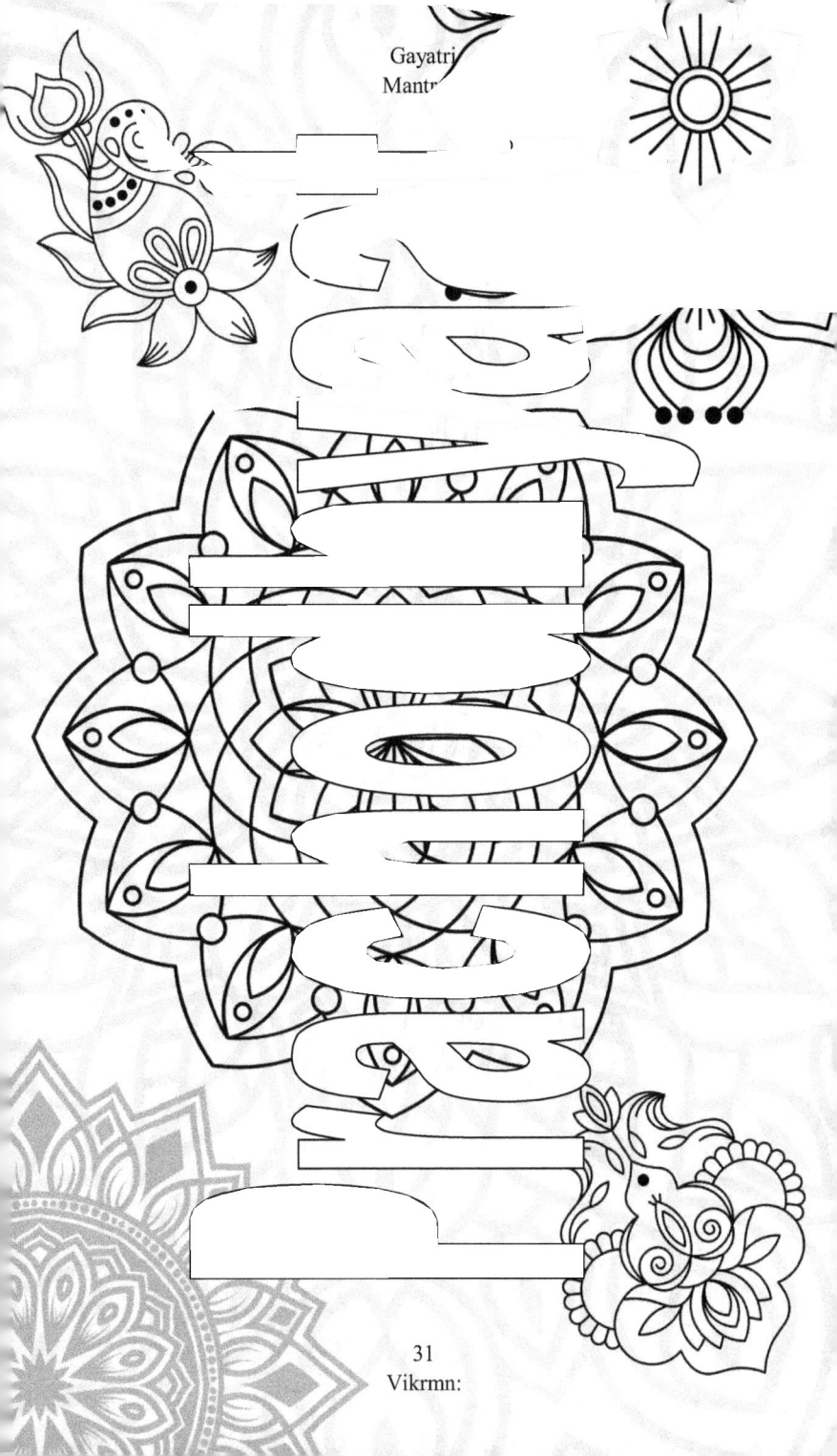

Do you want to
publish your artwork
on the cover page
of next edition
of this book?

Design a cover for this book
with your artwork
and post it on Instagram
tagging the Author.

The best entry will be
published in the next edition
of this book with the name
of the contributor.

--

-

*Mantras
are all about
observing,
learning,
evolving,
and passing
the wisdom
on to next
generation.*

--

About the Book

Gayatri Mantra is the most profound and powerful mantra that should be introduced to children and youth at an early age. But it gets difficult due to diminishing average attention span and rising screen time per day.

"**Gayatri Mantram Coloring Book**" bridges the gap between the spiritual essence and learning of the Mantra. It resonates deeply with young hearts, opening doors to both artistic expression and profound spiritual understanding.

Embark the children and youngsters on a captivating voyage to learn and explore the spiritual heritage of the Gayatri Mantra. This innovative fusion of tradition and creativity offers a harmonious blend, enriching their learning experience in a unique and engaging way.

--

About the Author

Vikrmn: is the author of many mind-bending and thought-provoking novels and self-help books that challenge preconceived notions creating a tapestry of profound wisdom.

Smiling Brahma, Krishna Crux, You by You, 10 Golden Steps of Life, Debit Credit of Life, and Guru With Guitar are a few of his widely quoted books.

Available on various social media channels, the author is reachable at www.vikrmn.com.